Music
Reference
Guide

k^{12}

Cover Image: © bluebearry/iStock/Thinkstock
Cover Design: Jayoung Cho

About K12 Inc.

K12 Inc., a technology-based education company, is the nation's leading provider of proprietary curriculum and online education programs to students in grades K–12. K^{12} provides its curriculum and academic services to online schools, traditional classrooms, blended school programs, and directly to families. K12 Inc. also operates the K^{12} International Academy, an accredited, diploma-granting online private school serving students worldwide. K^{12}'s mission is to provide any child the curriculum and tools to maximize success in life, regardless of geographic, financial, or demographic circumstances. K12 Inc. is accredited by CITA. More information can be found at www.K12.com.

ISBN: 978-1-60153-513-9 (online book)
ISBN: 978-1-60153-498-9 (printed book)

Printed by R.R. Donnelley & Sons Inc., Roanoke, VA, USA, June 2016

Contents

HOW TO USE THE PROGRAM

ADAPTING GROUP ACTIVITIES FOR ONE-TO-ONE SETTINGS

MUSIC THEORY

How to Use the Program

Welcome to *Spotlight on Music* from McGraw-Hill. *Spotlight on Music* promotes successful music learning as students explore and build foundational music skills. The program includes enriching musical experiences that help students understand music concepts. Students are exposed to a variety of interactive learning activities, such as focused listening, singing, creative movement, dancing, real and virtual instruments, authentic recordings, videos, music theory exercises, and playing the recorder (grades 3–8). *Spotlight on Music* provides opportunities for students to make meaningful connections with math, language arts, science, social studies, and other subjects.

This guide explains how to support students in this program. Review these pages to become familiar with the structure of *Spotlight on Music* and the accompanying resources.

Online Screens

This guide refers to several different screens that appear as you begin using the program.

MUSIC HOME PAGE

After you log in to your course, you will be redirected to the ConnectEd site for *Spotlight on Music*. Once there, select the box for your grade level.

Grade 1

Student Edition

Associated Course Content:
Grade 1

This screen appears.

MUSIC STUDIO MENU BUTTON

Select the button at the top left of the screen for the navigation menu.

LEFT NAVIGATION MENU

This screen appears.

UNIT AND LESSON SCREEN

Select the correct grade level at the top left of the screen, and choose the unit and lesson.

STUDENT LOGIN

The first time students enter *Spotlight on Music*, this message appears on the Music Studio home page.

Students should ignore this message. K¹² assigns the lessons that students should go to on any given day. To access lesson content,

1. Select the menu button at the top left of the screen.

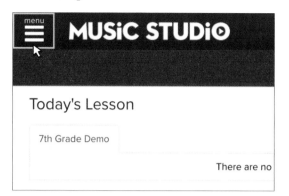

2. Select *Spotlight on Music* from the left side of the screen.

3. Select the correct grade level at the top left of the screen to open the unit and lesson.

4. Choose the assigned unit and lesson to access music content.

Spotlight on Music Instruction

Lesson plans in the Teacher Edition support instruction. They are designed to accompany student activities for high-quality learning experiences. Learning Coaches can follow these lesson plans as they work with students. Plans include direct instruction and guidance for moving through the music course.

K[12] teachers will share the lesson plans from the Teacher Edition with Learning Coaches.

Musical Instruments

Lessons in *Spotlight on Music* call for the use of musical instruments, including a tambourine and rhythm sticks, which K[12] provides. K[12] provides a recorder for students in grades 3–8.

When students are asked to perform a melody, harmony, or improvisation on a keyboard, piano, or other melodic instrument, they have the option of performing this melody on the recorder (grades 3–8), on a virtual keyboard, or with other virtual instruments in the course.

Students can access virtual instruments by selecting the Virtual Instrument activity in a lesson.

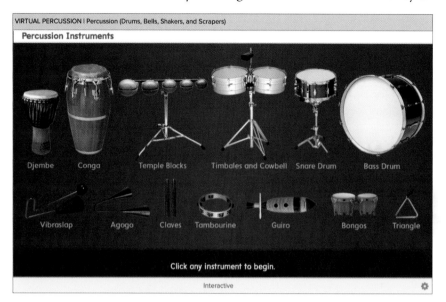

Students can also access a complete set of virtual instruments at the bottom of the Music Studio home page.

Spotlight on Music includes optional guitar lessons for grades 6–8. When students are asked to play a melody or accompaniment on the guitar, they may use their own guitar (if they have one) or a virtual guitar (fretted instrument) in the online program. **K^{12} does not provide a guitar for students in grades 6–8.**

Students can access different virtual guitars by selecting the Virtual Fretted Instrument activity in a lesson.

Students can also access the virtual fretted instruments at the bottom of the Music Studio home page. They may need to scroll to the right to find the guitars.

Music Resources

Spotlight on Music includes downloadable and printable resources, such as Song Anthologies with notation and lyrics, Resource Masters, Recorder Books, Guitar Books, Piano Accompaniments with movement suggestions, and Orff Orchestrations. There are two ways to access these resources.

- Left Navigation Menu

1. Select Resources from the left navigation menu.

All available resources within a grade level appear, including Song Anthologies, Resource Masters, Piano Accompaniments with movement suggestions, iSongs, listening maps, songs, Recorder Books, Guitar Books, audio and video, and more.

2. Select a resource for full access.

- Unit and Lesson Screen

  Choose lesson-specific resources from the unit and lesson screen.

The student view includes the following resources: Glossary of Instruments, Glossary of Music Terms, My First Italian Musical Words, Playing the Recorder, Playing the Guitar, and Keyboard.

Additional resources for Learning Coaches and teachers are available.

TEACHER AND LEARNING COACH RESOURCES

The Teacher Edition has detailed lesson plans and the following resources: Movement Glossary, Folk and Traditional Styles, Composers and Lyricists, Musical Instruments, and European Musical Styles.

MUSIC THEORY

Learning Coaches may need background in basic music theory and notation. This guide includes a section on music theory. The information is intended for reference purposes. Learning Coaches are not expected to read every entry in the music theory section of this guide.

RESOURCE MASTERS

Many lessons require students to complete Resource Masters (worksheets). Select the Resource Master icon in any lesson for access. Or, select Resources from the left navigation menu for access.

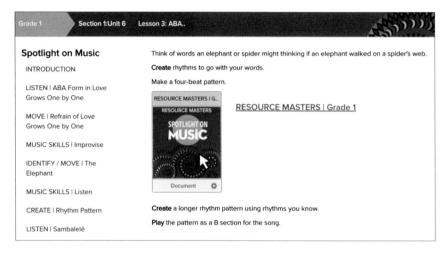

After the Resource Master opens, find the appropriate page, which can be downloaded and printed for student use. Resource Masters cannot be completed on-screen. Answer keys are at the end of the Resource Master.

PIANO ACCOMPANIMENTS AND MOVEMENT SUGGESTIONS

Many lessons reference the Piano Accompaniments for suggested movements. Select Resources from the left navigation menu for access.

RECORDER AND GUITAR BOOKS

There are three ways to find the Recorder and Guitar Books.

- Select the Book icon in a lesson.

- Select the Recorder or Guitar Book link in the Resources section on the Unit and Lesson screen.

- Select Resources from the left navigation menu, and then select the Recorder or Guitar Book from the menu.

MUSIC JOURNALS

Music Journals are an important part of the *Spotlight on Music* program.

PORTFOLIO | Music Journal

MUSIC JOURNAL | Adding Personal Style to Performances

Music Journal

What are some of the ways you can add your own personal
style to a performance of a song? What does your musical
interpretation say about who you are?

_____

_____

_____

_____

_____

_____

Interactive

Students can type directly in the interactive Music Journal screens by selecting the Music Journal activity to open it, but they will not be able to save their work. There are three ways to save Music Journals.

- Complete the Music Journal prompt in a Word or text document (instead of in the Music Journal activity) and save as usual.

- Copy and paste all text from the completed Music Journal into a Word or text document one line at a time.

- Right-click anywhere in the completed Music Journal, select Print, and save as a PDF or print a hard copy. The Music Journal activity must be open for print functionality.

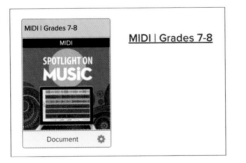

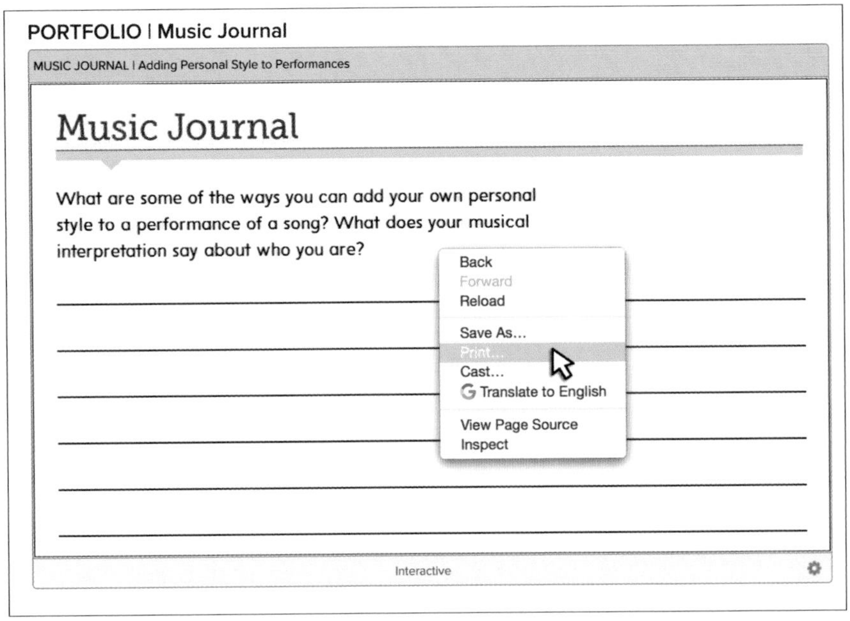

MIDI Activities

Some lessons in *Spotlight on Music* contain MIDI activities. K[12] implementation of *Spotlight on Music* does not include MIDI activities, so these activities can be skipped.

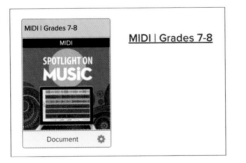

Assignment Time Lines for Grades 7 and 8

Not every activity in the *Spotlight on Music* program is required. To help students navigate to assigned activities, K[12] provides schedules for grades 7 and 8. The schedules outline the specific activities required for each lesson.

Adapting Group Activities for One-to-One Settings

Spotlight on Music was developed to provide high-quality music instruction in group settings and classrooms. Each lesson in the program includes detailed instructions for presenting music activities. These instructions are written with a classroom setting in mind and include references to "students" and "groups." For learning in a one-to-one setting, these instructions require some translation. The following adaptations are suggestions for using this program in individualized settings with one student.

Using This Program in Individualized Settings

When the text says . . .	use this text instead . . .	and do the following . . .
students	your student	Have your student do the activity.
groups	your student	Do the activity with your student, acting as a participant, if needed.
Give children an overview.	Give your student an overview.	Explain what's coming up.
Call on students. Ask students.	Ask your student.	Ask your student directly. Encourage multiple answers and discuss alternative ideas when appropriate.
Invite children to share. Invite the class to share.	Invite your student to share.	Have your student offer a response.
Invite children to listen.	Invite your student to listen.	Listen together.
Show children.	Show your student.	Show or demonstrate for your student.
Write down students' responses.	Record your student's responses.	Record your student's responses in a notebook.
Sit with students in a circle.	Sit with your student.	Find a comfortable, quiet spot with space for learning and moving.

(continued)

When the text says . . .	use this text instead . . .	and do the following . . .
Divide the class into groups.	Work with your student as a partner.	Be a responsive partner in this activity with your student.
Choose a student leader.	Have your student be the leader.	Encourage your student to take a leadership role, so you can follow along.
Who can point to? Who can show me?	Can you point to? Can you show me?	Ask your student directly and wait for a response.
Play in groups. Sing in groups.	Play with your student. Sing with your student.	Have your student play or sing a part on his or her own, or play or sing with your student. If there are multiple parts, such as a round or duet, play or sing one part, while your student plays or sings the other.

The following suggestions adapt specific types of activities for one-to-one use. With simple modifications, you can adapt group activities into meaningful and engaging one-to-one learning experiences.

General Guidelines for Music Activities

- Follow the instructions provided, which may include questions about specific music concepts.

- Encourage your student to be an active participant in music activities. Support engagement and take an active role yourself.

- As appropriate, invite your student to share background experiences or personal memories that relate to music and the concepts presented.

- Respond positively to your student's participation in music activities as your student develops concepts, skills, and music appreciation.

- Emphasize specific vocabulary and terms that accompany music activities. Reinforce language development while your student is engaged with music content.

- Be a model for your student, using target vocabulary, singing, clapping, and participating in music activities presented in lessons.

In the Spotlight (Intro Section)

- Introduce key vocabulary, concepts, and music in upcoming lesson(s). As appropriate, share helpful background information that relates to music activities.

- Use the provided Teaching Suggestions to expand on music content and make meaningful cross-curricular connections.

Group Activities

- For any games that require more than one player, be one of the players while your student assumes the role of the other player. If possible, invite a sibling or a friend to play selected games, so there will be more than two players.

- For role-playing situations that involve several parts, break down the activity and play as a twosome with your student. You may be able to play multiple roles.

- For explorations that refer to small groups of children, work one-to-one with your student. As appropriate, let your student take the lead. Be sure to talk with your student as you work together.

- For group projects, become your student's partner, contributing fresh ideas and materials in the process of producing a finished product or performance.

Music Making and Storytelling

- Enrich music-making experiences by adding physical actions or dramatization to support lyrics in music, as appropriate.

- For activities that call for specific physical movement, be an active participant, moving to music and demonstrating actions for your student.

- Encourage storytelling that relates to music activities. Support your student in retelling familiar stories and creating original stories. Contribute your own ideas to make storytelling more engaging, lively, and fun.

Guided Questioning

- Use open-ended questioning to encourage deeper thinking and greater responsiveness. Instead of asking questions that have a single answer, ask questions that can be answered in various ways. Include some questions that ask for opinions, and follow up with "Why do you think so?" Help your student construct thoughtful responses that make sense, but also have fun by allowing your student to share innovative ideas when formulating answers.

- Switch roles and give your student opportunities to pose questions, which promotes critical thinking skills. It also provides practice manipulating language and vocabulary that relates to target music concepts.

Activities Requiring Large Display Board

- If music activities require a large display board, use large paper, such as butcher block paper or freezer paper on a tabletop, along with markers or crayons.

- If available, use an easel with chart paper and markers, or use a dry-erase whiteboard with markers on a stand or tabletop.

Music Field Trips

- If possible, include opportunities outside the home that relate to music content. If local events are offered in your community, take your student to public concerts or music performances. Plan ahead and talk about where you are going and what you might hear or experience.

Music Theory

Reading and Writing Music: Pitch

This section includes background in basic music notation and information about **music theory** to help you guide students through the music course.

Tip: The text highlights key terms, which are defined at the end of this section.

MUSIC NOTATION

Music notation is music expressed in written form. The music staff is the canvas or backdrop on which notes and other music symbols are written. The staff is a musical map of high and low notes.

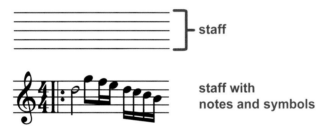

staff

staff with
notes and symbols

STAFF

The basic music staff has five lines and four spaces, counted from bottom to top. Music notes can sit on a line or in the space between two lines.

LINES AND SPACES

Pitch is the perceived highness or lowness of a sound. Each line or space on the staff represents a pitch. A single note is either on a line or in a space.

The first seven letters of the English alphabet—A, B, C, D, E, F, and G—make up the music alphabet. These letters are used to label the lines and spaces of the staff. The letters H–Z are not used in music.

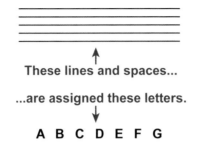

These lines and spaces...

...are assigned these letters.

A B C D E F G

CLEF

A music staff always has a symbol, called a **clef**, at the beginning of each line. The clef acts as a key to the musical code. A clef, which means "key" in French, assigns individual note names to specific lines and spaces, depending on where the lines touch the clef symbol.

treble clef   bass clef

The two most common clefs are the treble clef and the bass clef.

- **treble clef** the clef used by higher-sounding instruments to read music

- **bass clef** the clef used by lower-sounding instruments to read music

TREBLE CLEF

The treble clef is also called the G clef because the pitch assigned to the line that the clef wraps around is known as G.

NAMING LINES AND SPACES

Once you know how to read a clef and can identify one line or space on the staff, you can name the remaining lines and spaces. The name of the pitch on the space directly above the G line is A. The music alphabet only goes from A to G, so after G, the letter names start at A again. You can continue naming each line or space according to the music alphabet.

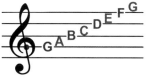

FOLLOWING THE MUSIC ALPHABET

To add note names on the lines or spaces lower than the G staff line, reverse the order and go backward down the music alphabet.

PITCHES ON THE TREBLE CLEF

Use these phrases to remember the lines and spaces of the treble clef.

For treble clef lines, **E**at **G**iant **B**reakfasts **D**uring **F**inals.

For treble clef spaces, **FACE**.

Select each letter on the staff.

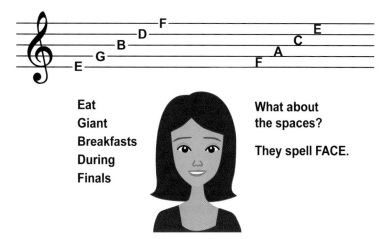

Eat
Giant
Breakfasts
During
Finals

What about
the spaces?

They spell FACE.

NOTE

The note symbol represents a particular sound that is played. Most music note symbols have a notehead and a note stem. You know which pitch to play based on where the note symbol sits on the staff. The example shows the note G because the notehead is centered on the G line.

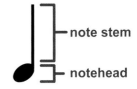

- **notehead** the round part of a music note that connects to the stem, or line, of the note

- **note stem** the line part of a note that extends away from the head, or round part of the note

NOTE NAMES

The diagram includes all the notes on the treble staff going up from one G to a higher G.

NOTE STEMS

The note stem flips when the notehead gets to the third line on the staff, which is B. The stem often changes direction on the third line of the staff to make the notes easier to read as they go up. However, the stem direction has no effect on the pitch.

LEDGER LINES

A basic music staff has five lines and four spaces where you can place notes to represent different pitches. But these five lines and four spaces do not cover all the different pitches that are available in music.

What happens when there are too many pitches to fit on the music staff? How do you represent pitches that are higher or lower than the staff? The treble staff goes up to a high G. Where do you place notes that are higher than high G?

You can extend the treble clef staff with ledger lines. Ledger lines are short horizontal lines that make it possible to add pitches that are too high or low for placement on the regular staff. Ledger lines above the staff are for high notes. Ledger lines below the staff are for low notes. Ledger lines extend the range of the music staff.

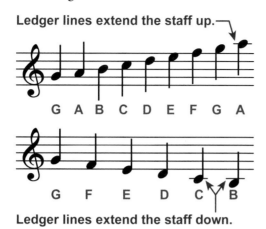

- **ledger lines** additional lines and spaces that extend the staff to include higher or lower notes

- **range** the span of notes an instrument can play or a voice can sing

If you only use the treble clef and keep adding more and more ledger lines for pitches that go lower and lower, the notes become difficult to read. For this reason, there are other clefs that make it easier to notate some instruments and voices.

BASS CLEF

The bass clef is used to write notes on a staff that are much lower than the notes in the treble clef. The staff line between the two dots on the bass clef is F, so the bass clef is also called the F clef.

Once you know where F is, you can continue identifying note names on each line or space of the bass clef staff according to the music alphabet.

F

F G A F E D C B A G

Tip: Use these phrases to remember the lines and spaces of the bass clef.

- For bass clef lines, **G**ood **B**oys **D**o **F**ine **A**lways.

- For bass clef spaces, **A**ll **C**ows **E**at **G**rass.

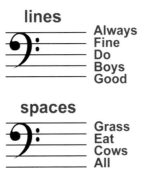

lines

Always
Fine
Do
Boys
Good

spaces

Grass
Eat
Cows
All

GRAND STAFF

The treble clef is used for higher-pitched instruments. The bass clef is used for lower-pitched instruments. When two staffs containing a treble clef and bass clef are combined, they form the **grand staff**. The treble clef and bass clef share a common note called **middle C**, which joins the two clefs.

grand staff

middle C

One treble clef staff and one bass clef staff joined by a bracket encompass a broad range of notes. Instruments with the greatest ranges, such as the piano and harp, use a grand staff.

The treble clef staff and bass clef staff can be spaced out to allow music notes to be written and read with ease; middle C on the lower staff is the same pitch as middle C on the upper staff.

Reading and Writing Music: Piano Keys and the Staff

KEYBOARD WITH TREBLE AND BASS TOGETHER

Pianists read music on the grand staff, generally playing higher notes in the treble clef (in blue) with their right hand and lower notes in the bass clef (in yellow) with their left hand. Middle C (in red) joins the two clefs.

Every line and space on the staff corresponds to a white piano key. The treble clef usually represents notes on the piano that start in the middle of the keyboard around middle C and move to the right. The bass clef usually represents notes to the left of middle C.

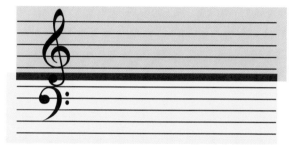

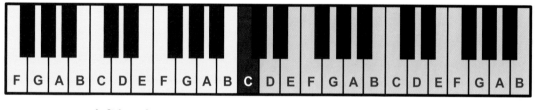

left hand   right hand

WHITE PIANO KEYS

It's important to become familiar with the piano keyboard because the keyboard layout is directly related to musical notation.

As you move to the right on the keyboard in the diagram, sounds are higher in pitch. As you move to the left, sounds are lower in pitch. The music alphabet used to label lines and spaces on the staff is also used to label each piano key. The letters of the music alphabet repeat after every seven white keys (A–G).

low   high

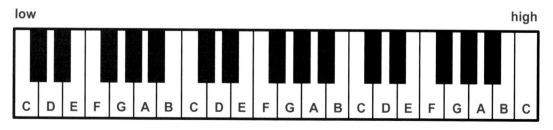

BLACK PIANO KEYS

Black keys on the piano keyboard are arranged in groups of two and three. The pattern of white and black in relation to the names of the keys always remains the same, as shown in the diagram. You can use that pattern to identify the white keys.

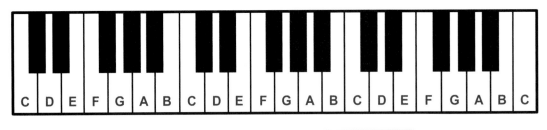

left hand   right hand

left hand   right hand

Because instruments have different ranges, they need different clefs. There is a third clef called an alto clef for certain instruments.

In an orchestra, the instruments follow this plan in music notation:

- The treble clef is used for high-range or higher-sounding instruments, such as the flute, trumpet, and violin, or the soprano voice.

- The alto clef is used for middle-range instruments, such as the viola.

- The bass clef is used for low-range or lower-sounding instruments, such as the bassoon, tuba, cello, and double bass.

ALTO CLEF

The range of a piano keyboard encompasses 88 pitches. Like the piano, the organ and the harpsichord use the grand staff. Some instruments use only one clef. High instruments like the flute or violin use only the treble clef, while low instruments like the cello or trombone use only the bass clef. Some instruments fall in the middle. These instruments use the alto clef. The **alto clef**, also known as the C clef, is used by middle-range instruments.

The viola, a middle-range string instrument, uses this clef so that its music notation requires fewer ledger lines. The alto clef looks like a B. The middle of the B indicates where middle C is.

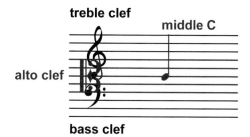

Once you have determined where middle C is on the alto clef, you can continue to identify note names on each line or space in the alto clef according to the music alphabet.

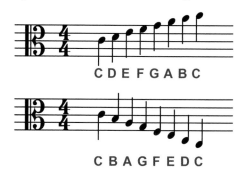

Reading and Writing Music: Rhythm

Music is much more than melodies or high and low notes. In addition to the melodic rise and fall of pitches within a song, what makes a song interesting, unique, and even catchy is the duration of each pitch within the song—the **rhythm**. Every note in a musical composition must start and stop.

Not only does music notation tell the exact pitch that a note should be, it also tells the length of time, or the duration of time, that a note should be played. Music notation can even represent periods of silence, when not to play notes.

In music, when you feel the **beat**, or a constant musical pulse, you are feeling a basic pulse that can speed up or slow down. The length of time that a music note is played is called its **note duration**. Note duration is specified using symbols called **notes**, which are shown in the diagram. Different notes represent different durations of time.

| whole note | half note | quarter note | eighth note | sixteenth note |

RHYTHM VALUES

WHOLE NOTE

The **whole note** has the longest duration of the notes in music. Just like a pizza can be divided multiple times to create smaller and smaller slices, a whole note can also be divided into smaller durations.

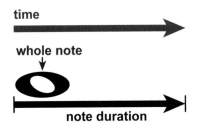

HALF NOTE

If a whole note is cut in half, the result is two half notes. The **half note** has half the duration of a whole note. Notice that the notehead of a half note is open like a whole note. However, the half note has a stem, and the whole note does not. In music, two half notes occupy the same amount of time as one whole note.

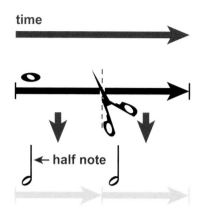

QUARTER NOTE

Just as a whole note can be cut in half to get two half notes, a half note can also be cut in half. When a half note is cut in half, the result is two quarter notes. Two quarter notes have the same duration as a half note. A single **quarter note** has one-fourth (or a quarter) of the duration of a whole note.

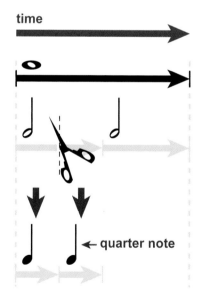

Four quarter notes take up the same amount of time as one whole note, and the same amount of time as two half notes.

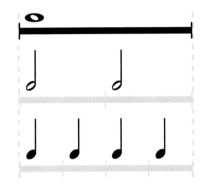

EIGHTH AND SIXTEENTH NOTES

You can continue to be divide notes to get **eighth notes** and **sixteenth notes**. Each eighth note is similar to a quarter note with a **flag** on the stem. Notes that are smaller in duration than quarter notes have flags. Each flag halves the value of the note it is attached to. Adding a flag to a quarter note cuts the value of the quarter note in half.

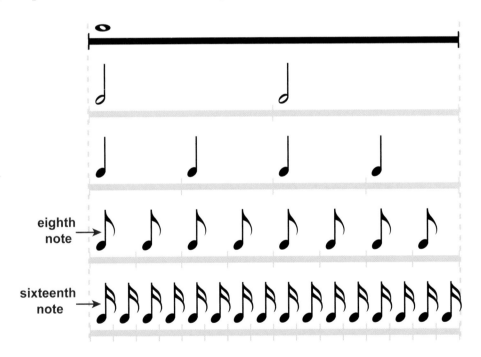

CONNECTING EIGHTH NOTES

When two eighth notes are side-by-side, you can write them as connected notes. The parallel line that connects the two eighth notes represents the single flag on each eighth note. Two connected eighth notes have the same rhythm duration as two single eighth notes that are side-by-side. They also have the same duration as one quarter note.

CONNECTING SIXTEENTH NOTES

You can connect sixteenth notes the same way as eighth notes. When sixteenth notes are side-by-side, you can connect them with two parallel lines to represent the two flags of each sixteenth note. Two connected sixteenth notes have the same rhythm duration as two single sixteenth notes that are side-by-side, which means they have the same duration as one eighth note.

STEADY BEAT

Just as you can feel the pulse or beat of your heart, you can feel the pulse in music. The pulse in a musical composition is called the **steady beat**. The steady beat is constantly in the background and guides clapping, marching, or simply moving to music.

HOW MANY BEATS?

You can assign the steady beat to a specific note duration, which tells you how long to hold each note in relation to other notes. If you make a quarter note equal to the steady beat and give each quarter note one beat, what beats do an eighth note and a sixteenth note have? According to the chart, if a quarter note is the steady beat, the eighth note is half a beat and the sixteenth note is one-fourth of a beat. Also, the half note has two beats, and the whole note has four beats.

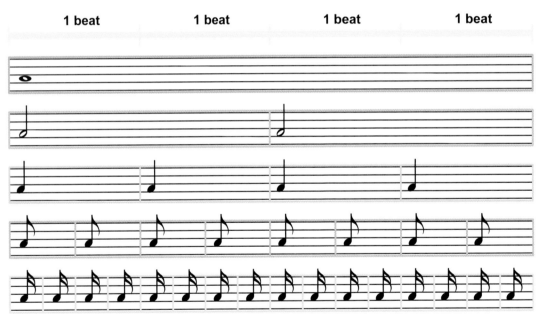

Note Duration

CLAPPING RHYTHMIC PATTERNS

You can help students clap rhythmic patterns using specific words. In music, when you see a quarter note, clap and say, "ta" (pronounced "tah"). When you see two eighth notes, clap and say "ti ti" (pronounced "tee-tee"). Two eighth notes have the same duration as one quarter note, so two eighth notes will take the same amount of time as one quarter note. You will need to clap and speak twice as fast for the eighth notes compared to the quarter notes. When you see a group of four sixteenth notes, say "ti-ri ti-ri" (pronounced "tee-ree tee-ree").

Keep in mind that the quarter note is still equal to the steady beat. Four sixteenth notes are equal to one quarter note, and each sixteenth note is half of one eighth note.

When a quarter note is doubled to create a half note, double the way you say and clap the note. The quarter note "ta" becomes "ta-a" (pronounced "tah-ah") for a half note. The whole note gets even more "ahs" added to it. When you see a whole note, clap and say "ta-a-a-a." The quarter note is still equal to the steady beat.

PAUSES IN MUSIC

Have you ever paused right before you were about to say something important or exciting, or right after you said something of great importance? Pausing before or after you speak can draw attention to and give weight to your words, and make your speech exciting and interesting to listen to. Similarly, music often includes pauses or rests. Rests are very important in music. They can give weight to the musical notes they come before or after, and add zest to an otherwise predictable passage.

RESTS

Consider the opening to *Eine Kleine Nachtmusik* by Wolfgang Amadeus Mozart. The portion in the diagram has three pauses identified by rest symbols.

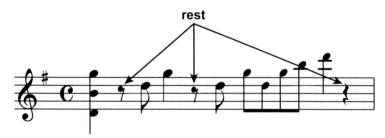

Just as music notes represent pitches and note durations in music, **rests** represent periods of silence in music. There are as many different kinds of rests as there are notes. For every note, there is a corresponding rest.

REST DURATION

When no pitches are played or sung in a piece of music, rests represent durations of silence. There is a rest symbol for each type of music note. For example, the chart shows that a quarter rest occupies the same amount of time as a quarter note. A quarter note indicates sound, while a quarter rest indicates silence.

Notes and Rests

	Whole	Half	Quarter	Eighth	Sixteenth
Note					
Rest					

QUARTER REST

Just like a quarter note is equal to one quarter of the duration of a whole note, a quarter rest is equal to one quarter of the duration of a whole rest.

When you clap musical patterns, do not clap on the rests. Clapping represents sound, so you do not clap on a rest, which indicates silence. You may find it helpful to say "rest" without clapping. Instead, open your hands so you don't make a sound. It is important to give the rest the correct duration of silence before clapping the next note.

HALF REST

When you double a quarter note, you get a half note. The same is true for a half rest. A half rest occupies the same amount of time as a half note. The half rest looks like a hat sitting in the middle of the staff.

When clapping a half rest, say "rest, rest" and open your hands so as not to make a sound. Make sure you are giving the half rest the correct duration of silence before clapping the next note.

WHOLE REST

Just like the whole note has the longest duration of sound, the longest basic rest is the whole rest. A whole rest occupies the same amount of time as a whole note. Depending on how many beats are in a measure, composers use a whole rest if there is no music in that measure.

When you see a whole rest in music, say "rest, rest, rest, rest" and open your hands so as not to make a sound. Make sure you are giving the whole rest the correct duration of silence before clapping the next note.

Tip: A whole rest is the same symbol as a half rest, but flipped upside down. Here's one way to remember the difference:

- A *whole* rest looks like a *hole* in the ground.

- A *half* rest looks like a *hat*—both *half* and *hat* start with the letter *h*.

SMALLER RESTS

Just like notes, a rest can have a flag to indicate duration. As a rest or note gets shorter in duration, another flag is added.

An eighth rest looks like a number seven. An eighth rest occupies the same amount of time as an eighth note. Just as two eighth notes are equal in duration to one quarter note, two eighth rests are equal in duration to one quarter rest. Just as a sixteenth note has two flags, a sixteenth rest has two flags.

Smaller Notes and Rests

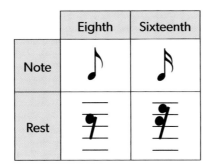

	Eighth	Sixteenth
Note	♪	♬
Rest	𝄾	𝄿

NOTE AND REST DURATIONS

A chart can help you understand relationships among different note symbols and their matching rests.

Rest Duration

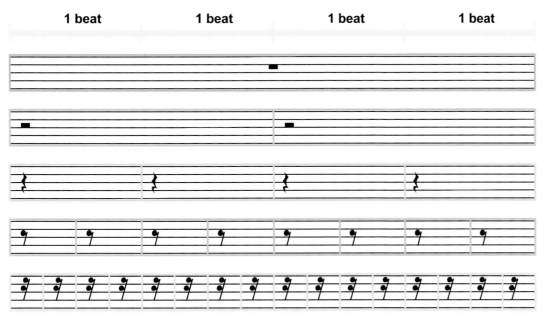

DOTTED NOTES AND TIES

A half note lasts half as long as a whole note. But what if a note lasts longer than a half note but not as long as a whole note? Is there a different symbol to represent that note duration? Yes. But rather than make up entirely new music symbols, simply add something to the symbols that already exist.

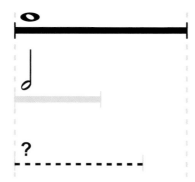

VALUE OF A DOT

A dotted note is just a regular note with a small dot to the right. A dot increases the note's duration by one half. How much is the dot to the right of the half note worth? Since a quarter note is half the duration of a half note, the dot is equal to one quarter note. A dotted half note is equal to one half note plus one quarter note.

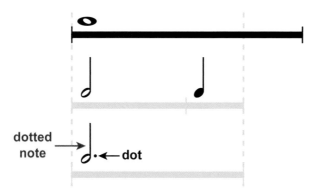

Tip: Adding a dot to any note adds half the value of the original note. A dotted half note is equal to one half note plus one quarter note.

DOTTED QUARTER NOTE

How much is the dot to the right of the quarter note worth? Since an eighth note is half the duration of a quarter note, the dot to the right of the quarter note is equal to one eighth note. A dotted quarter note is equal to one quarter note plus one eighth note.

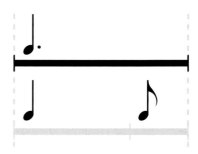

DOTTED EIGHTH NOTE

How much is the dot to the right of the eighth note worth? Since a sixteenth note is half the duration of an eighth note, the dot to the right of the eighth note is equal to one sixteenth note. A dotted eighth note is equal to one eighth note plus one sixteenth note.

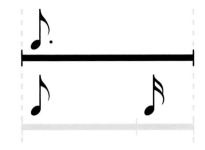

DOTS AND BEATS

Determining the equivalent value of a dotted note can take some practice. A dotted eighth note does not form a complete beat. A dotted eighth note is often combined with a sixteenth note to form the equivalent of one quarter note.

Dotted Note Duration

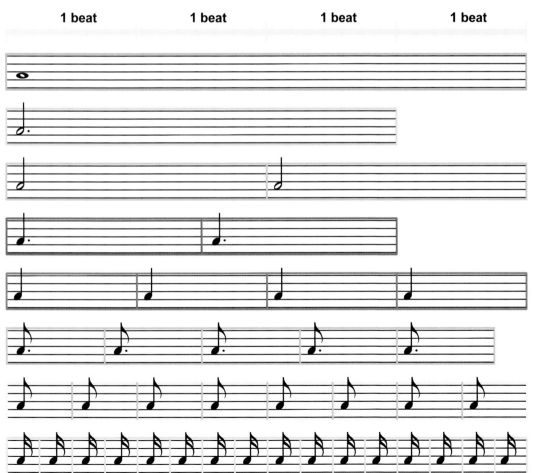

Dots are only one way to make notes longer. Ties also make notes longer. Ties join multiple notes of the same pitch to create one duration of sound. Ties are used to make the duration of a note to travel across a bar line, a straight vertical line that divides notes in one measure from another.

Tied notes are played by sounding the first note and holding the sound through the combined values of all tied notes. For example, if two quarter notes are tied together, they have the same duration as one half note.

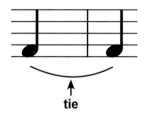

Reading and Writing Music: Time Signatures and Patterns

Notes in a musical composition are organized into patterns based on a specific beat, or rhythm. These patterns can be as simple as stripes on a tie or as complex as a finely woven quilt. Music notation uses different symbols that group notes to help a performer figure out the pattern.

TIME SIGNATURES

A rhythm is a sound pattern or an organization of note durations. There is a pattern in this group of notes.

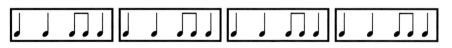

If you break up the notes into smaller groups with the quarter note acting as the steady beat, you can easily identify the four-beat pattern. The "ta ta ti-ti ta" pattern, which is boxed in the diagram, is made through basic repetition.

GROUPING NOTES FOR THE BEAT

If you group the notes, you can see the pattern more easily. In this example, with the quarter note as the steady beat, you can see another four-beat pattern. This time, the notes are arranged based on a specific number of beats in each group—four. In music, groups of notes are identified not with boxes, but with thin vertical lines, called **bar lines**.

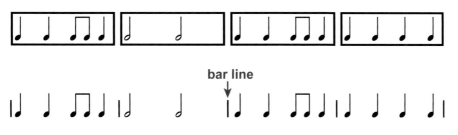

BAR LINES

Most musical beat patterns are organized into easily recognizable quantities. The area between two bar lines is called a **measure**. (Sometimes measures are referred to as bars.) It is easier to see how music notes are organized when they are grouped into measures. The musical system for organizing beats into measures is called **meter**. The example shows meter in both simple notes (top) and in a real music segment (bottom).

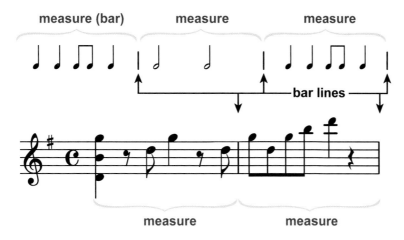

READING TIME SIGNATURES

Even though notes in a score are divided by bar lines and grouped into measures, you still can't tell how many beats are supposed to occur within each measure, or even the value of each note. That's where the **time signature** comes in.

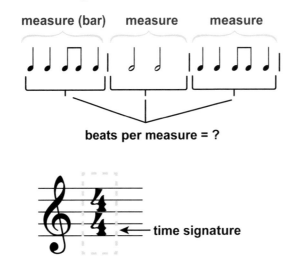

BEATS PER MEASURE

The top number of a time signature tells the number of beats in each measure.

The top number of this time signature is 4, which means there are four beats per measure.

The top example has two beats in each measure; the top number in the time signature is 2. The bottom example has three beats per measure; the top number in the time signature is 3.

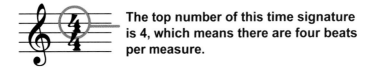

2 beats   2 beats

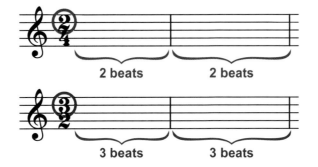

3 beats   3 beats

NOTE THAT GETS THE BEAT

The bottom number in a time signature specifies the type of note that receives one beat.

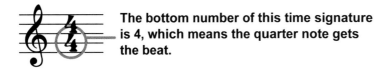

The bottom number of this time signature is 4, which means the quarter note gets the beat.

DIFFERENT TIME SIGNATURES

You are now ready to see how the numbers of a time signature work together.

4/4 TIME

In 4/4 time signature, also known as **common time**, the top number 4 means there are four beats in every measure. The bottom number 4 stands for a quarter note and indicates that the quarter note will get one beat. In this example, there are four quarter-note beats in every measure.

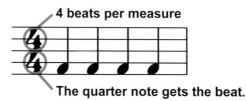

2/4 TIME

In this time signature, the top number 2 means there are two beats in every measure. The bottom number 4 represents a quarter note and indicates that the quarter note gets one beat. Since there are two quarter-note beats in every measure, this time signature is a 2/4 time signature.

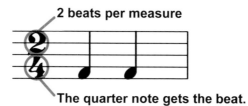

3/4 TIME

Here's another example where the quarter note gets the beat. In this example, the top number 3 means there are three beats in every measure, while the bottom number 4 means quarter note and indicates the quarter note will get one beat. So there are three quarter-note beats in every measure.

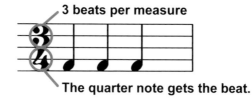

DUPLE, TRIPLE, AND QUADRUPLE METER

Beat patterns can be made up of different notes as long as the beats add up to the time signature. But why use different time signatures to organize the same type of notes? Why not use just one? Different time signatures or meters feel different. **Meter** is the musical system for organizing beats into measures, and each type of meter or time signature divides a measure into a certain amount of beats.

Simple meters can be duple (two beats per measure), triple (three beats per measure), or quadruple (four beats per measure). In simple meter, a natural accent or emphasis takes place on the first beat of each measure, which helps organize beats in your mind, as well as the way you feel the beat and rhythms of a song.

STRONG AND WEAK BEATS

In duple and triple meters, after the first strong beat of each measure, which is often referred to as the downbeat, the remaining beats in each measure are considered weak beats. In quadruple meter (such as the time signature 4/4), however, a secondary accent is given to the third beat.

The use of different time signatures and meters in music is why you feel rock music differently from polka music, even though both types of music use the same type of rhythmic notes. Composers select a specific meter for a piece of music depending on how they want the music to be heard and felt.

OTHER COMMON TIME SIGNATURES

Time signatures that have 4 as the bottom number are common time signatures, but they are not the only time signatures that exist. Here are the other common bottom numbers and what they mean.

- The number 2 indicates the half note gets the beat.

- The number 4 indicates the quarter note gets the beat.

- The number 8 indicates the eighth note gets the beat.

- The number 16 indicates the sixteenth note gets the beat.

3/2 TIME

Here is an example of a time signature where the half note gets the beat. The top number 3 means there are three beats in every measure, while the bottom number 2 means half note and indicates that the half note gets one beat. So there are three half-note beats in every measure.

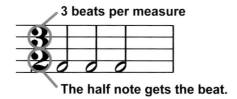

3 beats per measure

The half note gets the beat.

6/8 TIME

Here is an example of a time signature where the eighth note gets the beat. The top number 6 means there are six beats in every measure while the bottom number 8 means eighth note and indicates the eighth note will get one beat. A composer may use any combination of notes that add up to six eighth notes in each measure.

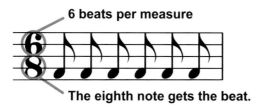

6 beats per measure

The eighth note gets the beat.

MORE TIME SIGNATURES

Here are a few more examples of different time signatures.

- The 4/2 time signature means there are four half-note beats in every measure (the half note gets the beat).

- The 5/8 time signature means that there are five eighth-note beats in every measure (the eighth note gets the beat).

- The 9/16 time signature means that there are nine sixteenth-note beats in every measure (the sixteenth note gets the beat).

Music covers a wide spectrum of speeds, pulses, beat accents, and rhythms, so different time signatures are useful.

The ends of measures are just as important as what is inside them. The measure line, or bar line, tells if the measure is special or just a plain old bar. The average bar begins and ends with a single bar line, which is how a measure will appear somewhere in the middle of a piece of music. There are a few instances, however, where they look different.

OTHER TYPES OF BAR LINES

Simply adding an extra line to the end of a measure to create a final bar line signifies that the piece is over.

The symbol that bookmarks a designated section to play again is called a **repeat sign**. A whole piece might be repeated, or just a few measures. One repeat sign goes at the beginning of the section, and the other is placed at the end. If an entire piece of music is to be repeated, there will be no repeat sign at the beginning of a section. You will see only one repeat sign at the end of the music.

How about a repeat sign and a final bar side-by-side? The measure with the number one is called the first ending, which tells the player to go back to the beginning. The next time around, the player will skip the measure with the number one, and go straight to the measure with the number two, or the second ending, to finish.

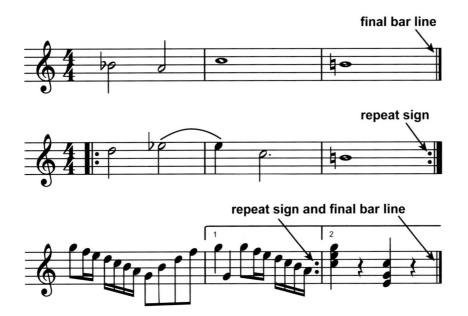

Understanding Music: Scales

Patterns are everywhere in music. You see patterns in measures that repeat with the same number of beats, bar after bar. You hear a rhythmic pattern in the beat of a drum.

The natural counterpart of rhythm is melody. Rhythmic patterns emerge from a beat combination, and melody patterns are often made up of notes in a **diatonic scale**. Jazz trumpeters who improvise a melody can do so because of a deep understanding of scales and patterns derived from those scales. Electric guitarists who rattle off a solo have scales under their command. Understanding scales is essential for any musicians who want to be creative. Whether they compose with pen and paper or spontaneously jam onstage, musicians use melody patterns as raw material for making fresh sounds.

THE PIANO KEYBOARD

A piano keyboard can help you visualize notes on the music staff. Each piano key corresponds to a note on a music staff. The white keys and black keys help differentiate between natural notes (white keys) and sharp and flat notes (black keys). Counting only the white keys on a piano, there are seven notes from C to C (counting both Cs as one note). Counting both white and black keys on a piano, there are 12 notes from C to C (counting both Cs as one note).

lowest octave   **middle octave**   **highest octave**

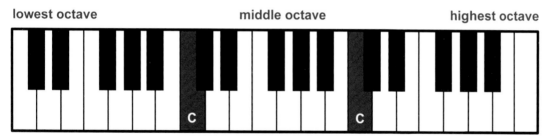

This notation shows how the white keys from middle C to C look when written on a staff.

This notation shows how the white and black keys from middle C to C look when written on a staff.

CHROMATIC SCALE

The 12 notes from C to C (counting both Cs as 1 note) make up the **chromatic scale**. The distance from one C to the next is an **octave**. The notes for the black keys on the piano are signified by the use of symbols called sharps or flats.

Look at the notated chromatic scale. The lines and spaces are used more than once. Even though a black key note is on the same line or space as another note, it does not share the same pitch or sound the same. The sharp symbol indicates a different sound or pitch.

HALF STEPS AND WHOLE STEPS

The distance between any two notes in music is called an **interval**. The distance from one note to another on the chromatic scale is called a half-step interval. A half step is the smallest interval in **tonal music**; tonal music has a definite pitch center and an organized relationship among its tones.

A half step occurs between a white key and a black key or between two white keys when there is no black key between them. When two half steps are combined, you have a whole-step interval. To find a whole step, move two keys from your starting point.

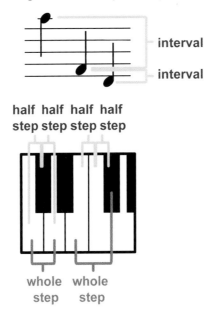

ACCIDENTALS: SHARPS

A **sharp** is used to identify notes sounded by black keys. On the staff, the symbol ♯ is placed in front of the note to make the note sharp. A sharp raises a note by one half step (or one piano key to the right).

Look at the black key between C and D. To move up one half step from C, you add a sharp to the note C. The name of the key and corresponding note becomes C sharp, or C♯.

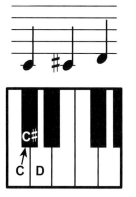

A sharp is one of five notation devices known as accidentals. An **accidental** is a symbol used to raise or lower a pitch by one half step, or sometimes two.

ACCIDENTALS: FLATS

The second type of accidental is the flat. A **flat** lowers a note by one half step (or one piano key to the left). On the staff, the symbol ♭ is placed in front of the note to make the note flat. The D becomes a D flat. To move down one half step from D, you add a flat to the note D. The name of the key and corresponding note becomes D flat, or D♭.

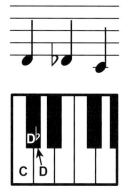

ACCIDENTALS: SHARPS AND FLATS

A black key can have two different note names, depending on whether a sharp or flat is used to name it.

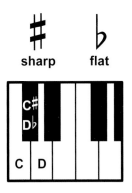

WHEN THERE IS NO BLACK KEY

On the piano keyboard, there is only a half step between E and F because no black key separates them. However, a sharp or a flat can still be added to raise or lower either of these notes.

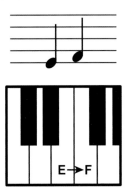

If a sharp is added to the note E, the note is raised one half step and becomes an E sharp. Notice how E sharp is the same key called F. This key can have two different names (E sharp and F), just like the black keys.

The staff shows notes E, E sharp, and F. The second and third notes are actually the same, even though they look like they should be different. A sharp raises the note that it is assigned to by a half step, and E is only a half step away from F.

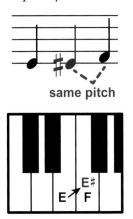

FLAT WHEN THERE IS NO BLACK KEY

A flat only lowers a note by a half step, so F, lowered by a half step, is either F flat or E. Therefore, the second and third notes on this staff are the same note.

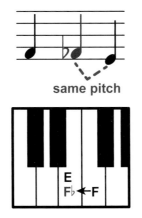

ENHARMONICS

Each black key and some white keys can be called by two different names. It's important to remember that, regardless of how it's written, the note will sound the same. When the same pitch has multiple names, they are called enharmonic spellings. A note's enharmonic is its name in sharps if it starts as a flat, or its name in flats if it starts as a sharp.

For example, the **enharmonic equivalent** of B flat is A sharp, and the enharmonic equivalent of A sharp is B flat. The same piano key is played for either B flat or A sharp. These two notes are enharmonic equivalents—two different names for a single pitch. Musical context will make it clear which name is appropriate. Once you have an understanding of accidentals, half steps and whole steps between notes can be easily identified. You can use a keyboard to identify whole and half steps between notes.

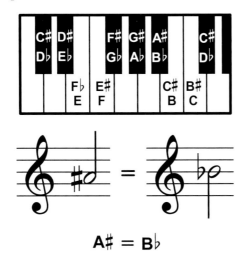

Tip: Notes that are a half step apart are next to each other, and notes that are a whole step apart have one key in-between them.

NATURAL SYMBOL

Musical notation has a symbol (♮) that is used to end accidentals that are no longer needed. It is called a **natural**. A natural cancels out any sharp or flat and returns a note to its original white-key name on the piano.

natural

For example, if a G sharp is followed by a G without a sharp, then a natural symbol is added to cancel the sharp. The natural symbol lowers the note by a half step. It works the same for flats, but in reverse. The natural symbol raises the note by half a step.

SUMMARY OF ACCIDENTALS

Accidentals are only good for the measure in which they first appear. After a bar line, all notes revert to their original pitch, based on the key signature.

Accidentals

Accidental	Effect	Where Played on Piano
sharp (♯)	raises sound of note a half step	one key to the right
flat (♭)	lowers sound of note a half step	one key to the left
natural (♮)	cancels sharps and flats	the white piano key associated with its staff position

SCALES

For centuries, musicians have grouped notes into scales. Those scales are then used to create songs. Scales give every note in a piece of music purpose. The notes of a scale help shape the sound of a piece of music and can determine whether the music will sound happy, sad, full of tension, or relaxed.

A scale is a series of adjacent notes that either ascend or descend. Because a series of notes can begin at any pitch, there can be many different scales. Most scales fall into a few common categories.

The interval between any 2 of the 12 notes of is a half step. All other scales in tonal music are created from the notes of a keyboard's chromatic scale. However, not all scales are made up of just half-step intervals.

MAJOR SCALES

Any **major scale** is made up of five whole steps and two half steps, arranged in this pattern, where W = whole step and h = half step: W W h, W W W h.

Look at how this major scale pattern appears on the staff, beginning with the note middle C. The major scale pattern of W W h, W W W h is the same no matter what major scale you are playing. Notice that the two half steps correspond to the white piano keys that don't have a black key between them.

SCALE DEGREE

Every note in a scale can be identified by its note name or by a number from 1 to 8, also known as its **scale degree**. In this example, C is scale degree 1, D is scale degree 2, and so on.

When referring to a scale degree, a number has a small carat symbol on top, as you can see at the top of the staff. The note on which a scale begins is always scale degree 1. The scale degree 8 is really scale degree 1 repeated in a new octave.

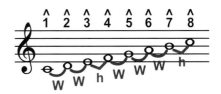

TONIC

A scale is always named for the note on which it begins. The example you just looked at is a C major scale because it begins and ends on C. The starting note is called the **tonic**. The tonic is the first and last scale degree in any scale. In tonal music, this note sounds like a resting point.

C Major Scale

tonic

C MAJOR SCALE

C major is a unique scale because it uses no sharps or flats. On the piano, this scale is represented by playing white keys only. If you were to add an accidental to any note on the scale, the pattern would be altered and you would no longer have a major scale.

The C major scale is easy to build on the piano beginning with any C key. The W W h, W W W h pattern is built right into the white keys when starting on C.

Scales don't have to start on C; they can start on any note. Here the major scale pattern begins on A flat to create an A flat major scale. Note how flats are used in the W W h, W W W h pattern.

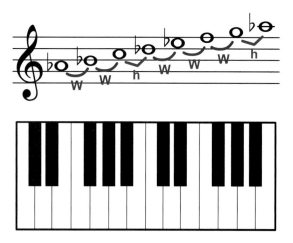

E MAJOR SCALE

The major scale pattern begins on an E to create an E major scale. Note how sharps are used in the W W h, W W W h pattern.

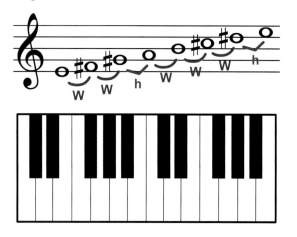

Tip: The name of a scale is the same as the name of the first note of the scale.

MINOR SCALES

In a major scale, the pattern of intervals is W W h, W W W h, which is easily seen on a piano with the C major scale. You can also play a **minor scale** on the piano without using any black keys: the a minor scale. Minor scales often sound sad or ominous.

Tip: The letter names of minor scales and chords are often lowercase to differentiate them from their major scale counterparts, which have letter names that are often uppercase.

The a minor scale has the same notes as the C major scale. However, where the C major scale starts on C, the a minor scale starts on A. The special term for two scales that are related in this way is relative. C major is the **relative major** of a minor, and a minor is the **relative minor** of C major.

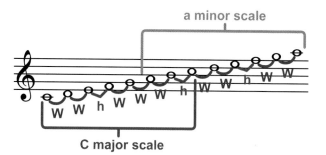

Starting on a note other than C means the pattern of whole steps and half steps must change to accommodate a minor scale. The natural minor scale formula is W h W, W h W W.

a MINOR SCALE

The a minor scale is easy to build on the piano beginning with any A key because the pattern (W h W, W h W W) is built right into the white keys when starting on A, similar to the major scale pattern built into the white keys when starting on C.

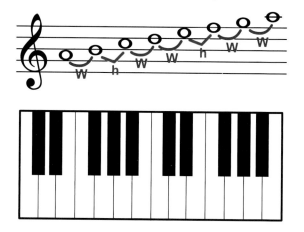

e MINOR SCALE

In the same way that major scales don't always start on C, minor scales don't have to start on A. They can start on any note. Building the minor scale pattern beginning on an E creates an e minor scale. Note how one sharp is used in the W h W, W h W W pattern.

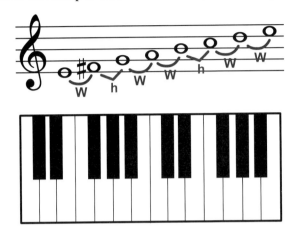

f MINOR SCALE

The f minor scale shows how the natural minor scale pattern is built into the scale. Note how flats are used to ensure that the W h W, W h W W pattern is correct in the natural minor scale.

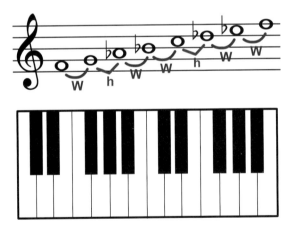

TYPES OF MINOR SCALES

Unlike the major scale, which is always the same, there are three different types of minor scales. The most basic is the natural minor scale. The two other types of minor scales, which are derived from the natural minor scale, are the harmonic and melodic minor scales.

HARMONIC MINOR SCALE

To convert any natural minor scale to a **harmonic minor** scale, the seventh scale degree is raised by one half step.

The seventh scale degree is raised by one half step.

MELODIC MINOR SCALE

To convert any natural minor scale to a **melodic minor** scale, both the sixth and seventh scale degrees must be raised by one half step. When the sixth and seventh scale degrees are raised, the minor scale pattern is once again changed and a new pattern emerges: W h W, W h W W.

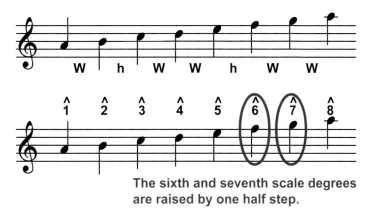

The sixth and seventh scale degrees are raised by one half step.

Tip: Melodic minor scales are played as a melodic minor scale when they are ascending and as a natural minor scale when they are descending.

RELATIVE MAJOR AND MINOR SCALES

Every major or minor scale has a relative minor or major scale. The C major scale and the a minor scale are considered relative major and minor scales because they share the same notes.

To figure out the name of the relative minor to a given major scale, count down two notes from the top note of the major scale. The top note of any diatonic scale is the eighth scale degree, so the sixth scale degree is the name of the relative minor.

From C major, count down one note to B and then then a second note to A. The a minor scale is the relative minor of the C major scale.

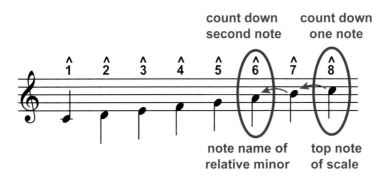

From G major, which has one sharp (F sharp), count down two notes from the top of the G major scale to reach e minor. The minor scale beginning on E also has only one sharp, on scale degree 2.

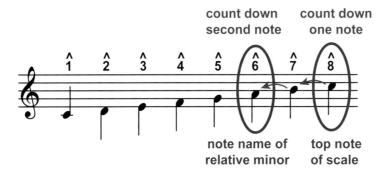

Major and minor scales do not differ much. They are constructed from the same sequence of notes; the big difference is the starting point.

Understanding Music: Key Signatures

Just like the symbols on a map key help you read a map, there are different symbols in music that act as keys to reading musical notation.

- Clefs assign individual note names to specific lines and spaces on the staff.

- Note symbols assign different durations to each tone.

- Time signatures tell how many beats a note should get and how many beats are in a measure of music.

Clefs, note symbols, and time signatures are not the only symbols for decoding musical notation. **Key signatures** tell which notes in a composition should be played as sharps or flats.

Most major and minor scales require accidentals on certain notes to establish the correct whole-step, half-step pattern. If a composer wants to write a song using the notes in a particular scale, she would need to write the accidental next to certain notes every time they appear, which could get cumbersome to both read and write. Key signatures solve this dilemma.

The **key** of a song is established by the notes in a major or minor scale. A key signature is a list of every accidental found in a major or minor scale. Key signatures are used so that composers do not have to write an accidental each time a certain note within a scale appears in a piece. Key signatures appear at the beginning of every line of music. Flats or sharps (but not both) appear in a single key signature, just like flats or sharps (but not both) appear in a major or minor scale.

key signature

FROM SCALES TO KEY SIGNATURES

The C major sale does not have any sharps or flats, so the key signature for C major would also not have any sharps or flats. To demonstrate how to transfer the accidentals from a scale to a key signature, use the A major scale, which has three sharps, and apply the major scale formula W W h, W W W h to build the scale.

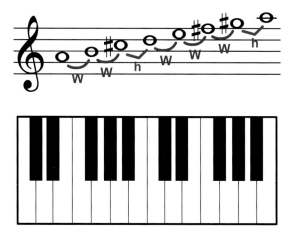

A MAJOR KEY SIGNATURE

The A major scale has three sharps: C sharp, F sharp, and G sharp. If you wanted to write a song using an A major scale, instead of writing a sharp next to every C, F, and G in the song, you could simply add those sharps at the beginning of each line of music, forming your key signature.

If you saw this key signature at the beginning of a song with a C sharp, F sharp, and G sharp, you would know you are in the key of A major and all notes on the lines or spaces for C, F, and G would be played as C sharp, F sharp, or G sharp.

Tip: A key signature is a list of all sharps or flats necessary to establish a major or minor scale. The notes in the scale that form the key signature establish the key of a song.

E MAJOR KEY SIGNATURE

Use the major scale formula W W h, W W W h to build an E major scale. The scale establishes the key signature and has four sharps: F sharp, G sharp, C sharp, and D sharp. If you want to write a song using an E major scale, instead of writing a sharp next to every F, G, C, and D in the song, you could simply add those sharps at the beginning of each line of music.

Tip: If you saw a key signature at the beginning of a song with F sharp, G sharp, C sharp, and D sharp, you would know you are in the key of E major and all notes on the lines or spaces for F, G, C, and D would be played as F sharp, G sharp, C sharp, and D sharp.

b MINOR KEY SIGNATURE

Just as key signatures can be formed from the sharps or flats in major scales, they can also be formed from the sharps or flats in minor scales. Use the minor scale formula W h W, W h W W to build a b minor scale. The scale establishes the key signature and has two sharps: C sharp and F sharp. If you want to write a song using a b minor scale, instead of writing a sharp next to every F and C in the song, you can add those sharps at the beginning of each line of music.

Tip: If you see a key signature at the beginning of a song with an F sharp and C sharp, and you know you are in a minor key, you know you are in the key of b minor and all notes on the lines or spaces for F and C should be played as F sharp and C sharp.

ORDER OF SHARPS

When putting the sharps from the scales into the key signatures, you do not put them on the staff in the same order that they appear in the scale. Sharps are always arranged in a special order for key signatures: F sharp, C sharp, G sharp, D sharp, A sharp, E sharp, B sharp. You will never have a C sharp without having an F sharp first, or a D sharp without having an F sharp, C sharp, and G sharp first.

Tip: Use this phrase to remember the order of sharps: **F**ast **C**ars **G**o **D**riving **A**round **E**very **B**end.

IDENTIFYING SHARP KEY SIGNATURES

Although the sharps in a major scale determine the sharps of a key signature, it would be difficult to memorize all the sharps in every major scale to determine the key signature. To determine what major you key you are in when there are sharps in the key signature, go up one half step from the last sharp to end up on the name of the key signature.

Key of D Major

FLAT KEY SIGNATURES

Key signatures can be composed of sharps only, flats only, or have no accidentals at all. Flats in a scale are transferred to a key signature in the same manner as sharps.

B FLAT KEY SIGNATURE

Use the major scale formula W W h, W W W h to build an F major scale. The scale establishes the key signature and has one flat: B flat. If you want to write a song in F major, instead of writing a flat next to every B in the song, you could simply add the flat to the beginning of each line of music.

Tip: When you see the key signature with a B flat at the beginning of a song, you know the key signature is F major. All notes on the lines or spaces for B will be played as B flat.

A FLAT KEY SIGNATURE

The A flat major scale has four flats: A flat, B flat, D flat, and E flat. To write a song using an A flat major scale, instead of writing a flat next to every A, B, D, and E, you could simply add those flats to the beginning of each line of music.

Tip: When you see the key signature with an A flat, B flat, D flat, and E flat at the beginning of a song, you know the key signature is A flat major. All notes on the lines or spaces for A, B, D, and E will be played as A flat, B flat, D flat, and E flat.

ORDER OF FLATS

In the same way that sharps are put in a specific order for sharp key signatures, flats are put in a specific order. Flats appear on the staff in the opposite direction as sharps. If sharps appear on the staff in the order F sharp, C sharp, G sharp, D sharp, A sharp, E sharp, and B sharp, then flats appear on the staff in the opposite order of B flat, E flat, A flat, D flat, G flat, C flat, and F flat.

Tip: Use this phrase to remember the order of flats: **B**ig **E**lvis **A**lways **D**elivers **G**uitar **C**hords **F**ast.

IDENTIFYING FLAT KEY SIGNATURES

To determine what major key you are in when there are flats in the key signature, look at the next to last flat in the key signature. That's the name of the key.

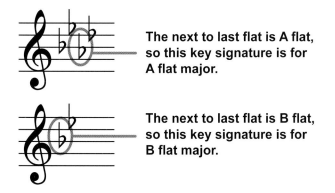

The next to last flat is A flat, so this key signature is for A flat major.

The next to last flat is B flat, so this key signature is for B flat major.

The only exception to this rule is the key of F major, which has one flat. Since F major only has one flat, you can't look at the next to last flat in the key signature. F major containing one flat, B flat, is a key signature you have to memorize.

MINOR KEY SIGNATURES

There are fifteen key signatures that represent the possible major scales, seven sharp key signatures, seven flat key signatures, and one key signature with no sharps and no flats. Each key signature that is associated with a major scale can also be associated with a minor scale.

When a major scale and a minor scale share the same set of sharps or flats, they are called the relative major or the relative minor of each other. For example, C major and a minor both do not have any sharps or flats.

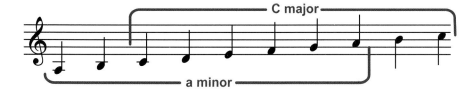

IDENTIFYING MINOR KEY SIGNATURES

A minor scale starts three half steps below the first scale degree or tonic (starting pitch) of its relative major scale. The first scale degree or tonic of a minor scale will always be three half steps below the tonic of its relative major scale. The minor tonic is also the sixth scale degree of its relative major's scale. You can use this knowledge to determine a minor key signature as long as you know the name of the major key signature.

F MAJOR'S RELATIVE MINOR

To find the name of F major's relative minor, count backward three half steps from the first scale degree of F major, or count to the sixth scale degree of F major. That's also the name of the minor key signature. You can see that when you count back three half steps from the first scale degree in the F major scale, or if you count to the sixth scale degree of the F major scale, you land on the note D. The relative minor of F major is d minor, and the minor name of the key signature with one flat is d minor.

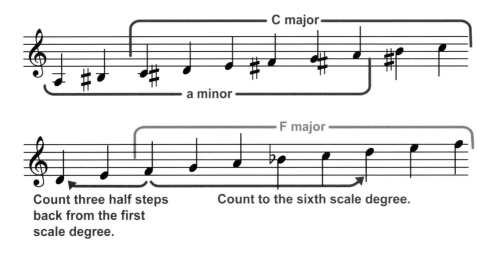

Count three half steps back from the first scale degree.

Count to the sixth scale degree.

IS IT MAJOR OR MINOR?

Since minor and major keys share key signatures, it may seem difficult to tell whether the key signature is representing the major scale or minor scale. If you are unable to listen to a piece of music to determine whether it is in a major key or minor key, look at the last measure. Usually, the last note or chord of a song has the tonic note or first scale degree in it. If the last note or the lowest note in the last chord of the song matches the name of the major key signature, then the song is probably in the major key. If the last note or the lowest note in the last chord of the song matches the name of the minor key signature, then the song is probably in the minor key.

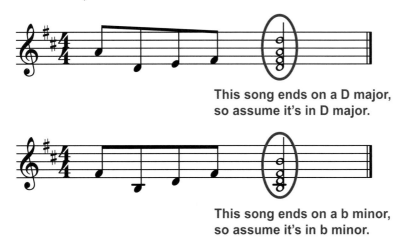

This song ends on a D major, so assume it's in D major.

This song ends on a b minor, so assume it's in b minor.

Understanding Music: Diatonic and Chromatic Notes

Every major or minor scale has an identifying key signature, indicated at the beginning of a music staff. The key signature determines the notes that will occur naturally within a piece of music, and the notes that will occur as sharps or flats. A note that occurs naturally within a piece of music or that belongs to the scale that is used in the composition is a **diatonic note**. A note that is raised or lowered by a half step to make it outside of the given scale or key used in the composition is a **chromatic note**.

The key of C has no sharps or flats, so any chord that you play in the key of C will also have no sharps or flats. The diagram shows the notes that are diatonic notes and those that are chromatic notes.

This note is chromatic because it is not found in the key signature. A sharp outside of the key signature was added to the note.

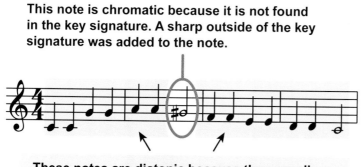

These notes are diatonic because they are all found in the key of C major, the key of this piece.

Tip: Don't confuse chromatic notes with the chromatic scale. The chromatic scale is a list of all pitches in an octave. These chromatic notes are notes that are not included in the major or minor scale that will form a key signature.

NOTE C

The note C is central in learning music. The C major scale has no sharps or flats, so it's the easiest to play on the piano. The note middle C sits in the middle of the grand staff and the middle of the piano keyboard. C is the key signature around which all others are centered. Because the C major scale has no sharps or flats, you can also say that the key of C major has no sharps or flats.

You have learned to build major scales starting on any note, using the formula W W h, W W W h. To understand the relationships of key signatures to each other, examine at the G major and F major scales, along with C major.

C MAJOR, G MAJOR, AND F MAJOR SCALES

The G major scale has one sharp, while the F major scale has one flat. Therefore, the key of G major has one sharp, and the key of F has one flat. These notes were not arbitrarily selected to have one sharp and one flat, respectively, in their scales and keys. Examine the logic involved to figure out how scales and key signatures all relate to each other.

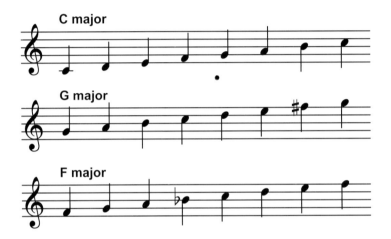

AN IMPORTANT INTERVAL

On the piano keyboard, count up or down five white keys from C to get to G or F. The distance between the C and G keys or the C and F keys is called a **perfect fifth**. On the staff, the ascending scale notates the five white keys on the piano keyboard spanning from middle C up to G. The descending scale notates the five white keys on the piano keyboard, spanning from middle C down to F.

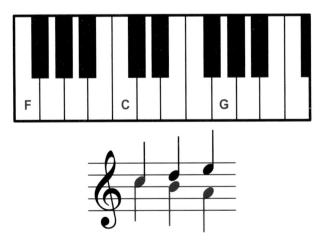

There is only one sharp in a G major scale and only one flat in an F major scale. When you begin on the note C and move up an interval of a perfect fifth (or five white keys to the right), you land on the note G, which is the tonic note of the scale with one sharp: G major. When you begin on the note C and move down an interval of a perfect fifth (or five white keys to the left), you land on the note F, which is the tonic note of the scale with one flat: F major.

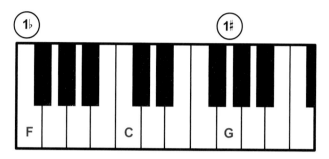

INTRODUCING THE CIRCLE OF FIFTHS

In music, when you leap an interval of a perfect fifth, you get to leap one major key, too. If you go up the piano keyboard, you'll end up with sharp keys. But if you go down, you'll end up with flat keys. Instead of looking at a keyboard, you can look at the **circle of fifths** and see the same thing.

Here's how the circle of fifths works:

The key of C, with no sharps or flats, sits at the top of the circle of fifths. If you move up or down an interval of a fifth from C, you land on G and F. The keys G and F, which only have one sharp and one flat, respectively, sit directly to the right and left of C. G sits on the right to show the notes going up a fifth, while F sits on the left to show the notes going down a fifth. Going up a fifth adds sharps, while going down a fifth adds flats.

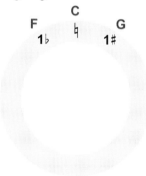

If you move up an interval of a fifth from G, you land on D. The key of D has two sharps. If you move down an interval of a fifth from F, you land on B flat. The key of B flat has two flats.

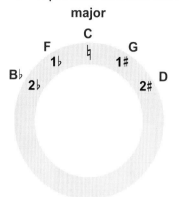

You can continue moving up or down an interval of a fifth on each side of the circle of fifths to continue adding key signatures, increasing the number of sharps or flats in each key signature by one each time.

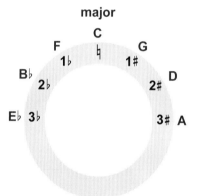

When you continue counting up by a perfect fifth, you will end up with a total of seven sharps on the right side of the circle. When you continue counting down by a perfect fifth, you will end up with a total of seven flats on the left side of the circle. The bottom three signatures on the circle of fifths are enharmonic notes. These key signatures will sound the same.

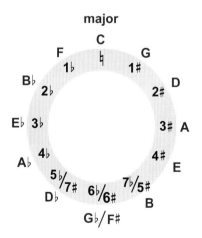

THE COMPLETE CIRCLE OF FIFTHS

Not only does the circle of fifths pattern work for major key signatures, but as you can see, it also works for minor key signatures, starting with a minor at the top of the circle. The complete circle of fifths is a chart detailing all of the major and minor key signatures and the pattern in which to build them. It is used to visually show the relationship between the keys. It is an important tool to help understand and identify key signatures, find relative major and minor keys, and remember the order of sharps and flats in key signatures.

REVISITING THE ORDER OF SHARPS AND FLATS

The sharps and flats are ordered in a logical way in a key signature. The circle of fifths helps you understand why sharps and flats are ordered as they are.

Seven possible sharps are added, one at a time, as you move from key to key around the circle of fifths. In G major, the key with only one sharp, the sharp symbol is always placed on the fifth line, F, to show that the note that gets a sharp in G major is F. In D major, the key with two sharps, there are sharp signs on F and C. A major, the key with three sharps, has sharp signs on F, C, and G. Sharps appear in key signatures in the same order they are added in the circle of fifths.

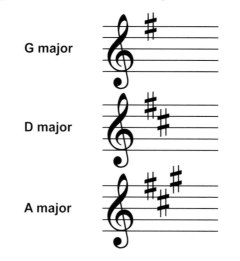

Flats appear in key signatures in the opposite order of sharps. However, flats also appear in key signatures in the same order they are added to the circle of fifths.

Understanding Music: Music Parameters

If every note in a piece of music were played at the same volume with the same execution, and if every song were performed at the same tempo, music would not be very interesting. It would be difficult to feel an emotional connection to the music.

When composers write music, they do more than determine the duration and pitch of each note in a composition. They also determine how loud or soft they want a note or a group of notes played, how they want a note presented, and what speed they want the music performed. Composers can easily describe all of these different elements of music through the use of **music parameters**. There are three important parameters in music: tempo, dynamics, and articulation.

TEMPO

The speed of a piece plays an important role in determining the mood of a piece of music. Think about the song "Happy Birthday." You know how fast it normally goes. Try to imagine the same song with the same words, but performed very slowly. It creates an entirely different feeling. Or picture a funeral march, ordinarily quite slow and stately, performed at breakneck speed. It certainly wouldn't mean quite the same thing.

Tempo is the speed at which a song is played. Every song has a constant pulse called a steady beat. When the steady beat in a song gets faster or slower, a change in tempo occurs.

tempo = how fast

When composers write a piece of music, they usually decide on the tempo they would like the music to be performed. Tempo has a huge effect on the feeling and mood of a piece. When choosing a tempo for a piece, a composer thinks about the mood that a tempo will create for the listener. While some music has a slow tempo, some music requires a fast tempo to evoke an appropriate mood, feeling, or reaction. Tempo plays a big role in the excitement and energy of a piece.

Composers pay close attention to tempo when writing their pieces because of the effect that tempo has on the feeling and mood of the music. It is important, therefore, that they give musicians specific directions for how fast or slow to play a piece.

EXPRESSIONS IN MUSIC

Music has its own set of symbols to represent certain actions and sounds. When tempo markings were first introduced, Italian music and culture were so dominant in the European scene that they set the standard for the international vocabulary of music. Hundreds of years later, people still use Italian terms to describe many musical instructions.

Italian terms used to describe the tempo in a piece of music not only characterize the tempo, but they are often used to name a **movement** in a piece, a self-contained part of a larger musical work. In addition to establishing the tempo, these terms give some insight into the mood of the piece.

Italian Tempo Terms

Italian Term	Meaning
grave	very, very slow and solemn
largo	very slow
adagio	at ease; quite slow
andante	at a walking pace
moderato	at a moderate pace
allegro	fast, cheerful
presto	very fast
vivace	lively and fast
prestissimo	as fast as possible

ESTABLISHING A TEMPO

Italian terms provide a general idea of tempo, but there are times when more precision is needed. Time signatures tell which note gets the beat—often a quarter note. You can figure out the actual time value of a note in a piece by using metronome markings (MM). The metronome was perfected by the German inventor Johann Mälzel in the early 1800s. The MM seen in music to indicate a metronome marking comes from Mäzel's metronome. **Metronomes** help musicians keep consistency of tempo when playing a piece, and they allow several players to synchronize their tempi. The marking MM in a score comes from Mäzel's metronome.

METRONOME

A metronome ticks like a clock to keep a steady beat. A clockwork mechanism inside makes the bar swing back and forth, clicking, at a speed determined by the movable weight. The closer the weight moves to the bottom, the more clicks you hear per minute. The higher up the bar, the fewer clicks per minute because the bar has to move through more space. Electronic metronomes click out the necessary number of beats. If you do not have a metronome, you can find a virtual metronome online.

METRONOME MARKINGS

Metronome markings (MM) are placed at the beginning of a piece of music. They are measured in beats per minute (BPM). They tell how many beats should be played in the space of one minute.

If you see the following at the top of a piece of music, the music will have 60 quarter notes in one minute, or one every second.

$$\quarternote = 60$$

If you see the following at the beginning of a piece, the music will have 220 quarter notes in one minute.

$$\quarternote = 220$$

CHANGING TEMPO

Composers establish the tempo for a piece of music using both Italian terms and metronome markings. They often want to change the tempo during the piece, and they use specific instructions to do that.

If composers want to speed up the tempo of a piece from where the current tempo is, they use the marking *accelerando*. However, if composers want to gradually slow down the tempo of a piece from where the current tempo is, they use the marking *ritardando*. If composers want to return to the original tempo of the piece, they use the marking *a tempo*.

DYNAMICS

A song's **dynamics** is how loud or soft music is. As composers and arrangers write and orchestrate music, they think about which part is the most important at what time. They may use dynamics to highlight those parts. Composers rarely use one dynamic level throughout an entire piece.

dynamics = how loud

DYNAMIC MARKINGS

There are dynamic markings for different levels of loudness and softness. When instruments are played louder or softer, or when there is a change in how many instruments are played at the same time, a dynamic change occurs. Skillful changes in dynamics can change the mood of performances in an instant.

PIANO AND FORTE

The dynamic terms are only approximate. When notating dynamic changes, composers use Italian terms, as with tempo and other markings. The main categories for dynamics are loud and soft, or *forte* and *piano*. Dynamic terms expand to indicate very loud (*fortissimo*) or very soft (*pianissimo*). The word *mezzo* is added to indicate medium (*mezzo forte* and *mezzo piano*). Though these terms and abbreviations are used the most often, composers sometimes use *ppp* or *pppp* and *fff* or *ffff* to indicate extremely soft or extremely loud.

Italian Dynamic Terms

Italian Term	Abbreviation	Meaning
pianissimo	*pp*	very soft
piano	*p*	soft
mezzo piano	*mp*	medium soft
mezzo forte	*mf*	medium loud
forte	*f*	loud
fortissimo	*ff*	very loud

Sometimes composers may want to create a very sudden change in dynamics, so they pair the word *subito* with one of the dynamic markings. For example, suddenly soft would be *subito piano*, and suddenly loud would be *subito forte*.

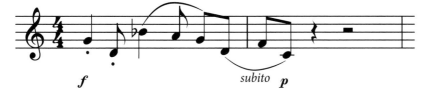

CRESCENDO

Although sudden changes in volume can be exciting, gradual changes in volume can not only be exciting, but can evoke other emotions as well.

The term **crescendo** indicates a gradual increase in volume. The symbol for *crescendo* is a hairpin opening to the right either directly above or directly below the notes it is intended for. To play a *crescendo*, each note from left to right included in the *crescendo* would be played louder than the previous note.

DIMINUENDO OR DECRESCENDO

The term **diminuendo** or **decrescendo** tells a performer to get gradually softer.

The symbol for *decrescendo* is a hairpin opening to the left either directly above or directly below the noteheads it is intended for. To play a *decrescendo*, each note from left to right included in the *decrescendo* would be played softer than the previous note.

ARTICULATION

Articulation is how crisp the notes are. You might sing the song "Row, Row, Row Your Boat" by singing each note quickly, like you are poking it with a pin. Or you might sing the song smoothly by holding each note fully and letting go only when it is time to sing the next note. It would take the same length of time to sing the whole song either way, but the song would sound very different. Composers use this same technique in their musical compositions to add interest and excitement to their music.

articulation = how crisp

ACCENTS

When composers want to emphasize one note more than another, a dynamic change may not be sufficient. Articulating a note in a particular way can help accomplish this. Performers can emphasize a note by playing it more loudly than the notes around it, which is called an accent. An accent is marked by placing a > symbol above or below a note head. If an accent is needed that is stronger than a typical accent, a **sforzando** ("forced" accent) is used.

The mark **sfz** indicates a *sforzando*.

STACCATO

Music notation in which notes have a dot underneath them, are detached and slightly shortened when they are sounded, is called **staccato**. Placing a *staccato* dot above or below a note ensures that the note is not connected to the note immediately following it.

LEGATO

Sometimes notes are purposefully connected in a smooth and flowing manner. **Legato**, the opposite of *staccato*, is an articulation in which notes are played smoothly with no separation between them. The first two notes are played *staccato*; however, composers then add a slur above the next several notes, indicating that the notes should be played smoothly and connected, or *legato*.

Key Terms

accelerando becoming faster; speeding up

accidental a symbol used to raise or lower a note by one or two half steps; Examples include sharp, flat, natural, double sharp, and double flat.

alto clef the clef used by middle-range instruments to read music

articulation a music parameter describing how crisply or smoothly a note or series of notes should be played

a tempo an instruction to return to the original tempo after some deviation from it

bar lines straight, vertical lines that divide notes in one measure from another; also referred to as measure lines

bass clef the clef used by lower-sounding instruments to read music; It is also called an F clef because its two dots surround the F line on the staff.

beat a constant musical pulse

chromatic note a note that is raised or lowered by a half step to make it outside of a given scale or key

chromatic scale a scale that includes all 12 notes contained in an octave

circle of fifths a graphic diagram where any pair of adjacent pitch names represent the interval of a perfect fifth, showing all major and minor key signatures and the relationships between them; used to construct the sharp and flat keys of all 12 notes in the chromatic scale

clef a musical symbol placed at the beginning of the staff, indicating which pitches will be represented by the lines and spaces of the staff

crescendo gradually becoming louder

diatonic note a note that belongs to the scale that is used in the composition where it is located

diatonic scale a scale with seven different pitches arranged in order from lowest to highest or highest to lowest; Examples include the major and minor scales.

diminuendo or **decrescendo** gradually becoming softer

dynamics a music parameter describing the changes in volume of a piece of music

eighth note a note having an eighth of the duration of a whole note

enharmonic equivalent a note that sounds at the same pitch as another note but has a different name

flag an extension of the note stem to show rhythm value

flat an accidental that lowers a note by a half step

grand staff one treble clef staff and one bass clef staff joined by a bracket to encompass a broad range of notes; used by instruments with the greatest ranges, such as the piano and the harp

half note a note having half the duration of a whole note

harmonic minor a natural minor scale with the seventh scale degree raised by one half step to create a leading tone

interval the distance between any two notes

key the pitch relationships that establish a single note as the tonal center or key note (tonic note) with respect to the other pitches, creating the major or minor scale upon which a song is based; The first note of a major or minor scale (the tonic note) is the name of the key.

key signature an arrangement of sharps or flats at the beginning of a music staff that specifies which notes are in the scale to be played

ledger lines additional lines and spaces that extend the staff to include higher or lower notes

major scale a scale consisting of the following five whole-step intervals (W) and two half-step intervals (h): W W h, W W W h

measure a segment of notes in a particular beat pattern

melodic minor a natural minor scale with the sixth and seventh scale degrees raised by one half step to create a leading tone

meter a musical system for organizing beats into measures; is defined by a time signature

metronome a device used for establishing tempo in music

minor scale a diatonic scale consisting of the following five whole-step intervals (W) and two half-step intervals (h): W h W, W h W W

movement a self-contained part of a larger musical piece

music notation music expressed in written form

music parameters ways to measure the elements of music

music theory the development of methods to analyze the elements of music; also refers to the study of the history of analysis of music

natural an accidental that cancels a previous sharp or flat symbol

note duration the length of time that a music note is played

notehead the round part of a music note that connects to the stem, or line, part of the note

octave two notes with the same name that are five whole steps and two half steps apart

perfect fifth the interval of three whole steps plus one half step

pitch the perceived highness or lowness of a sound

quarter note a note having a quarter of the duration of a whole note

range the span of notes an instrument can play or a voice can sing

relative major a major scale or key that shares the same number of sharps or flats with a minor scale or key located one-and-a-half steps higher

relative minor a minor scale or key that shares the same number of sharps or flats with a major scale or key located one-and-a-half steps higher

repeat sign the sign that marks a particular section of music to be repeated one or more times

rest a pause, or an interval of silence, in a measure of music; Rests are represented by symbols that mark a certain duration of time.

rhythm a regular pattern of sounds and beats in music

ritardando slowing down gradually

scale degree a number that identifies the position of a note in a scale

score a music manuscript

sharp an accidental that raises a note by a half step

sixteenth note a note having a sixteenth of the duration of a whole note

steady beat the pulse in a musical composition

stem the line part of a note; extends away from the head, or round part, of the note

tempo a music parameter that describes the speed, or varying speeds, at which a piece of music should be played

time signature a two-number sign placed at the beginning of a composition defining how many beats are in a measure and what note is equal to one beat

tonal music music with a definite pitch center that has an organized relationship among its tones

tonic in music, the first and last scale degree in any scale; In tonal music, this note sounds like a resting point.

treble clef the clef used by higher-sounding instruments to read music; It is also called a G clef because the pitch assigned to the line that the clef wraps around is known as G.

whole note a note having the longest duration in music